Adopt

A Challenge to the Church

Sarah L Lamb

Methodist Student Minister, Cranmer Hall, Durham

GROVE BOOKS LIMITED
RIDLEY HALL RD   CAMBRIDGE   CB3 9HU

Contents

1   Introduction 3

2   Biblical Insights into Family and Adoption 4

3   The Myth of the Christian Family 8

4   Who is Available for Adoption? 11

5   Who Wants to Adopt? 14

6   Who Takes the Decision? 17

7   Creating the Right Family: An Eschatological Model of Family 21

8   Conclusions 23

    Bibliography 25

    Notes 26

Acknowledgements

I would like to thank Dr David Clough at Cranmer Hall, Durham who first encouraged me to develop my thinking and research in this area and who then co-operated with Revd Dr Robert Innes in providing incisive comments as this booklet was written. I would also like to thank my husband, Andrew, and our two sons, without whose existence my passion for family life and adoption, in particular, would be a far smaller part of who I am.

The Cover Illustration is by Peter Ashton

First Impression July 2003
ISSN 1470-854X
ISBN 1 85174 535 1

Introduction

1

Statistics about children in Local Authority care make grim reading. In March 2001 the number of children in such care was 58,900, 65% of whom were in foster placements and 11% in children's homes.[1]

According to MORI, in October 2001, 14,000 children had been in care continuously for more than 5 years and 5,000 children were waiting for a suitable adoptive family.[2] The present government has stated its intention to increase the numbers of adoptive parents and reduce the numbers of children in Local Authority care and, after considerable debate, the Adoption and Children Act was passed in November 2002. The Act made it possible for any one person or couple over the age of 21, and a resident of the UK for more than a year, to become an adoptive parent provided that they were deemed 'suitable' and, if relevant, their relationship was 'stable and permanent.'[3] These statistics and the recent legislation form the backdrop to this booklet and its call for the church to respond to the plight of children who wait to be adopted.

In encouraging a serious consideration of the adoption of children, out of care and into loving families, this booklet is a challenge to Christian voices who spoke out in the debate preceding the Adoption and Children Act, voices who focussed on restricting the range of potential adopters rather than on the needs of children in care. It is a challenge to Christian ministers, social workers and adoption agencies to raise the awareness of adoption in our churches and, by so doing, to help create families that offer a new paradigm for the Christian family in contemporary society.

Adoption has been marginalized as an answer to a personal initiative rather than as a response to an external need

Adoption happens when a child who is not born to a family becomes a full member of it. Adoption transforms and creates a family, and yet it remains on the margins of Christian family life. Christian adoption agencies obviously work within the same legislative frameworks as secular agencies, but the distinctive principles and values that first brought Christian agencies into being are less evident nowadays, and most agencies are indistinguishable from one another. Christian couples who are unable to have their own children may consider adoption and could opt for infertility treatment. Rarely do existing families with children adopt further children. Adoption has been marginalized as an answer to a personal initiative rather than as a response to an external need.

This booklet begins by examining what the Bible says about the family and adoption. The Bible shows us that the notion of extending the family beyond natural, blood relationships existed for the people of Israel in the Old Testament. In the New Testament the Christian understanding of family emphasizes the value of loving one another irrespective of status or age. From this point, I reflect upon ideas of what it is to be a Christian family, before examining the evidence concerning who is available for adoption and who wants to adopt. I also consider the work of adoption agencies, since they have the responsibility and the power to decide who should adopt. Having looked at these aspects of adoption, I finally propose that Christians should affirm a new understanding of what it is to be a family, an understanding which firmly encourages and supports adoption.

2 Biblical Insights into Family and Adoption

Old Testament

The whole of Scripture is underpinned by the work of the Creator described in Genesis 1–2. Man and woman are created in the image of God. In Genesis, God created a suitable 'helper' to be with Adam, creating a couple who would work co-operatively. Alongside the requirement for faithfulness to God, the Old Testament establishes a firm dependence upon the principle of creation and of fidelity in marriage, so that children can have a mother and a father who will be honoured by them, as per the fifth commandment (Ex 20.12). Man and woman, wife and husband are upheld as a model for mutual love and the place for the proper care for children. This is the biblical ideal.

There is no law or rite of adoption mentioned in the Hebrew Bible and no use of the word for adoption *huiothesia* (meaning 'adoption as son') mentioned in its Greek version, the Septuagint. There are, however, examples of activity resembling adoption (Gen 48.5–6; Esther 2.7, 15), and the early life of Moses is close to our contemporary understanding of adoption (Ex 2.10).

The Old Testament features a strong kinship model of family. The 'children of Israel' (Hosea 11.1) are one nation under God. The great patriarchs headed the formation of this group of Israel: Abraham and Sarah; Isaac and Rebekah; Jacob and Rachel. Within this very large grouping of 'children' were tribal groups of several hundred people, and within each tribal group there were other more immediate kinship groups, of maybe 50 to 100 people, tied by concerns of economic survival, property and inheritance. Within this unit, there was a strong sense of familial duty, often in connection with the preservation of the bloodline. If the eldest son should die without an heir, so the second son should take the widow as his wife and any male offspring would be considered as preserving the bloodline of the deceased son (for example Genesis 38). There is an echo of adoption here, where the birth parents are different from those accepted as parents.

The 'children of Israel' are one nation under God

The responsibilities and privileges of kinship form part of the backdrop to stories like Ruth. Yet alongside the stories of love and self-sacrifice, there are stories of jealousy and deceit within families (for example Esau and Jacob, Sarah and Hagar). Recognizable physical and emotional aspects of family membership existed within the people of Israel but they existed within in context where faithfulness to Yahweh was the priority. Barton writes that within Jewish monotheism 'the demands of God must always take precedence over everything and everyone else, even family.'[4]

Welcoming the stranger into the kinship group took time and effort

The kinship relationship led to large, extended families, who were nonetheless expected to be open to the needs of outsiders. The command to offer hospitality to strangers (for example Ex 23.9) occurs no less than 37 times in the Hebrew Bible. This extended the Levitical principle of loving your neighbour. You love your neighbour because they are like yourself, but you have to be *taught* to love strangers because they are *not* like yourself. Welcoming the stranger into the kinship group took time and effort. This sentiment, alongside the prophetic declaration of needing to give greater protection to the vulnerable, the widowed and the oppressed (Amos, Hosea, Isaiah) is part of the distinctive, Jewish cultural background to the ministry and teaching of Jesus.

Jesus and Family

Jesus' preaching of the kingdom of God created a tension with the duties and responsibilities of being part of a family. Jesus clearly gives his family of faith priority over his kinship family (Mt 10.32–9, 12.47–50; Mk 3.31–5; Lk 12.52–3, 9.61–2, 14.26). Blood connections such as parents and siblings are relationships that have less significance to a disciple than obedience to God. Family life has its own spiritual pitfalls. Family tensions are found in the home of Martha and Mary (Luke 10.38–42), as well as in the home of Jesus himself (Mk 3.21, 6.1–6a; Jn 7.5), and are a topic of his teaching in, for example, the parables of the two sons (Mt 21.28–32) and the prodigal son (Lk 15.11–32). In both cases there is a mixture of choice, honour and shame occurring side by side. Like the Old Testament, the New Testament does not sentimentalize families, and Jesus' 'hard sayings' stand in strong continuity with biblical and Jewish monotheism.[5]

Jesus used his knowledge of Scripture to uphold the real intention of the law, namely the honouring of one's mother and father (Mk 7.9–13). Whilst the presence of children is not specified as a reason for a husband and wife to remain married, Jesus' teachings do promote fidelity and permanence within marriage (Mt 5.31–2, 19.3–12; Mk 10.1–12). Jesus assumes that even fallible human parents will love and care for their children (Mt 7.9–11). He invokes children to help the disciples learn important lessons (Mk 9.33–7). And, very significantly, Jesus welcomes and blesses children (Mk 10.13–16). 'Whatever be the nuances of the recorded sayings of Jesus, the linking of the child to the activity of God in his kingdom represents a particularly unforgettable image. It contains a radical message in the reversal of the usual relationship of adult to child and represents a sharp re-evaluation of the pivotal social value of honour.'[6]

Paul, Family and Adoption

Paul's writings about the family can lend themselves to a particular view of family that features a hierarchy of authority and the subordination of some family members. Suffice it to say that those texts known as the 'household codes' (Col 3.18–4.1, Eph 5.22–6.9, 1 Pet 2.18–3.7, and also 1 Tim 2.8–15, 6.1–2, Tit 2.1–10) cannot be used to provide unequivocal support for 'family values.' Thus, James Dunn's study of the household codes concludes that: 'The relationships within the family and household were themselves part of Christian vocation and indeed, we may say, were the first place where responsibility to the Lord should come to expression and be put to the test.'[7] The early church family had the difficult task of being a paradigm for a new family structure. Paul asks for family and household ties to be transformed by Christ.

Paul uses the Greek word *huiothesia* (see above) on five occasions: Galatians 4.4–5; Ephesians 1.5; Romans 8.15; Romans 8.23; Romans 9.4. James Scott has found that the word *huiothesia* is one of the commonest terms of adoption employed in Hellenistic Greek.[8] He suggests that whilst Paul's use of the word as a technical religious term is without parallel, his meaning is equivalent to Greek non-religious usage. It is simply appropriating the normal usage of the word. In Roman culture the one adopted was likely to have been a slave, or son of a slave, within the household and, through adoption, the slave became both free and also heir to the estate.

Galatians 4.5 is the earliest occurrence in the Pauline corpus.[9] Scott explores a discontinuity between the legal illustration of guardianship in 4.1–2 and the application of adoption in 4.3–7. He harmonizes the verses by connecting the issue of slavery (heirs 'are no better than slaves') to the one experienced by Israel in Egypt. Now 'adoption as sons' (4.5) follows guardianship, as the liberation from Egypt in the Exodus followed after a time of slavery and bondage. Scott regards this new liberation as a second Exodus and sees it as an 'eschatological redemption.'[10] Adoption becomes the means of becoming children of God, where Christians experience redemption into 'a relationship with the Father established by "adoption."'[11] Paul now makes the logical deduction that the transformed relationship, confirmed by the in-dwelling of the Spirit, enables the children to call their Father 'Abba!'

The family that started with the relationship of the natural Son to the Father is extended through adoption

The family that started with the relationship of the natural Son to the Father is extended to include new children through adoption. The verses in Ephesians (1.4–5) speak of God's loving plan for each person and how our adoption, as part of his plan, brings him pleasure. In the age to come, we can be fully intimate with God and all reliance on blood ties will be replaced by bonds of love.

Romans 8.15 and 8.23 form part of Paul's explanation about the transforming and liberating work of the Spirit. Again the analogy is made with slavery, and there is a sense of the future as we await 'the redemption of our bodies' after adoption. We look forward to being part of the heavenly family. Paul's use of *huiothesia* in Romans 9.4 links with the Old Testament understanding of the Israelites being 'children of God' and the whole nation being one large family under God.

Paul's use of the word 'adoption' helps paint a picture of family that goes beyond physical, blood ties towards new ties of relationship that begin in the present and are continued within the family of God in the age to come.

3 The Myth of the Christian Family

Contemporary Christian understandings of the family are, of course, shaped not just by Scripture but by 2,000 years of church teaching and practice.

There is insufficient space to give an account of all this history here but some of the attitudes emerging in England, from the early to mid-seventeenth century are worth reflecting on. At this point, the ability of clergy to marry created a particular model of being a family, a model recorded at length by the Puritan English conduct book writers.[12] Parents had a duty to discipline their children and to literally beat the sin out of them. The authority resided in the male head of the household, women were subordinated and the upbringing of children was characterized by strong discipline. 'With the gathering of children and servants to hear the Bible, pray and be catechized, the holy household of early Stuart England achieved its most emblematic form.'[13] Boys had a harsh regime at home and at boarding school; girls were expected to be chaste, silent and obedient. A pattern of parenting emerged (certainly for the literate) that was regarded as being highly biblical, with children being subordinate to parents, where firm discipline was essential and home upbringing featured Christian education. 'There was a good deal of criticism of parents who were seen as slack in these duties.'[14] According to Anthony Fletcher, this is the legacy handed on to some strands of conservative evangelical thought in the church of today.[15] This is not to say that, what Francis Bridger has termed the 'conjugal nuclear family'[16] is not God's ideal, but it is a challenge to attitudes and expectations that have been created over the years and are now exist as a fixed idea about what a Christian family should be like.

> *Parents had a duty to discipline their children and to literally beat the sin out of them*

In the years following the Reformation, into the eighteenth century and more recently, it became possible to differentiate between Christian families according to denomination and theology. Within the Roman Catholic Church, for example, marriage and the family are 'part of the natural order given by God for the good of the marriage partners and for the procreation of children.'[17] Marriage is held to be sacramental. In its paper *Familiaris Consortio* (1981), 'On the Family,' the Roman Catholic Church stated that the family is rooted in marriage and is 'the foundation of society' with every member having equal dignity. In Methodism, as in Evangelical Anglicanism, marriage is not sacramental. Methodism has been pragmatic in responding to the realities of marriage and family life and, for example, Methodist ministers have been able to re-marry divorcees in church since 1946. For its part, the Methodist Conference of 1992 produced a general definition of the word family as

> used of a wide range of groupings of people, living in very different relationships and bound together in various ways. In our own society it is most often used of a couple and their children, if any—the so-called 'nuclear family.' These children may be theirs by birth, adoption, fostering or some other relationship of caring.[18]

Across the denominational spectrum some churches would hold positions characterized by certain theological standpoints. In brief, an evangelical stance would uphold marriage and family as symbols of social stability and moral virtue. A liberal view would play down the sacramental nature of marriage and develop a dialogue with contemporary experience and social sciences. A feminist critique of Christian tradition would find the home to be a source of oppression, sexual abuse and exclusion.

What is clear is that across the spectrum of Christian views on the family, different attitudes are deeply contentious. 'The family' easily becomes the focus for anxieties about marriage, or co-habitation, or same sex relationships, or oppression of women. Yet, amidst all these concerns, the church easily risks overlooking the astonishing priority given to children by Jesus. *Something to Celebrate* puts it like this: 'The command of Jesus, "Let the children come to me," is a symbolic gesture whose true meaning has yet to be embodied in the life of church and society. For we (and this is more true perhaps in Britain than in some other countries) have yet to learn how to give full welcome to our children in ways that protect them from abuse, allow their individual potential to develop, and induct them into the responsibilities of belonging to family and society.'[19] And, amongst all the debates about the construction of the family, it is particularly crucial that Christians do not sweep aside the needs and interests of children who have no family.

The church easily risks overlooking the astonishing priority given to children by Jesus

In a prevailing climate of angst regarding family life, Jon Davies has drawn attention to the possibility of the family becoming a source of liberation for those who experience instability. He hopes for 'a firm and loving restatement of the necessity of family life for children, for the poor and for society as a whole.'[20] This raises the issue of how the Christian family regards children who are not 'their own.' If they are regarded as subordinate to adults and needing to be kept under strict discipline, then children who have been abandoned by their adult creators may be seen as of very low value. As contemporary society abandons marriage and re-shapes the family into something unrecognizable to most Christians, then Christian people can easily set aside the victims of society's mistaken ways. Children can end up abandoned by both their birth parents and by the Christian family.

The reconstruction of the Christian family is what is required and a strong affirmation of all that it can offer to children

As Davies says, 'It is my belief that the deconstruction of the family is causing suffering... A church, a Christian community which contributes to this suffering is behaving sinfully.'[21] Gerard Loughlin echoes this view: 'The idea of the Christian family turns sour when it ceases to promote fidelity, mutuality and the dispossession necessary for the reception of children as gift, and instead becomes a means of attacking those whom it itself excludes and constructs as "threat."'[22] The reconstruction of the Christian family is what is required and a strong affirmation of all that it can offer to children. After all, family is both kinship and a family of faith, and 'Christianity challenges the assumption that the only real kinship is based on birth, biology and blood.'[23]

Who is Available for Adoption? 4

In recent centuries, there has been an emphasis on blood lineage together with an assumption that immoral behaviour might be inherited as 'bad blood.'

This led to orphaned or destitute children being routinely institutionalized. Such was the antipathy to parentless children, that a policy of forced emigration to the colonies was implemented from the 1920s onwards. This practice continued until 1967 when 90 children left for Australia.[24] Only the very fortunate were fostered. Arguments around 'bad blood' and inheritance delayed adoption legislation in England until the English Adoption Act 1926.[25] Even then, adopted children were unable to inherit legally until 1949.

Until the 1960s, 'birth outside marriage was the major reason for placing a child for adoption, due in the main to the stigma of illegitimacy, so that logically it was a married couple that was considered a suitable alternative.'[26] During this period, social workers attached to hospitals would link a pregnant woman with an adoption agency and develop a discussion about the future of a child she may not be able to care for herself. Abortions were illegal and were attempted at great risk to the pregnant woman. Despite this situation, adopted children were looked upon as second-class citizens, and the stigma of adoption led to damaging secrecy within families.

The peak year for adoption was 1968, with nearly 25,000 adoptions.[27] This date coincided with the passing of the Abortion Act (1968). Legitimate access to abortion, and the increasing use of the contraceptive pill, made prevention of unwanted pregnancy much easier. Generally, there was better welfare for single mothers, accompanied by a shift in societal attitudes supporting single parenthood. However, although social services departments encouraged single mothers to give up babies for adoption until the late 1970s, there was now an option for unwanted pregnancies to be legally terminated. The work of hospital social workers, whilst offering adoption as an option, increasingly developed into a counselling service about the lingering effects of abortion on the woman, who might regard the possibility of placing her unborn child for adoption as undesirable or inconvenient. The overall effect of these developments is that fewer and fewer babies have been available for adoption.

Nonetheless, the most recent statistics show some slight improvement in overall adoption numbers. The number of babies adopted in England in the year ending 31st March 2001 was only 210.[28] But, encouragingly, the total number of adoptions, of all children under 18, was up by 400 from the previous year to a total of 3,100. Most of this growth (75%) represented adoption of children in the age group 1 to 4 years. This increase may be due to the extra publicity the subject of adoption was given during the debates preceding the Adoption and Children Act (2002). Alternatively it may have resulted from activity following the Prime Minister's stated intention to increase the numbers of adopters by 40% by 2004.[29] Whatever the reason, it is vital that this upward trend is continued for the sake of children in care.

Why Children Need Adopting

A MORI poll conducted on behalf of the British Agencies for Adoption and Fostering (BAAF) in October 2002, found that there is a widespread misunderstanding about the reasons why children need adopting. There is a persistent myth that adoption occurs after family breakdown or the death of a parent. In fact, the main reason (39%) why children need adopting is because of abuse or neglect.[30] The poll also found a high level of awareness (41%) of overseas adoption. This might indicate that overseas adoption of, say, a baby, could present itself as a more obvious option to a potential adopter than adoption of a child from the UK care system. Despite an encouraging trend, prospects are not good for the thousands of children who wait to be adopted. One journalist wrote:

> More than 5,000 children under the age of 16 are in council care... According to Home Office statistics, they are 50 times more likely than their contemporaries to end up in prison, 60 times more likely to become homeless and far more likely to become drug addicts or prostitutes...Yet a child adopted in its first four years has almost the same chance as everyone else of going on to higher education and getting a job.[31]

This is corroborated by the Department of Health: 'Research shows that generally adopted children make very good progress through their childhood and into adulthood compared with children brought up by their own parents and do considerably better than children who have remained in the care system throughout most of their childhood.'[32] The reasons for the high numbers of children waiting for adoption include:

- Many children (as many as 40% publicized in the BAAF magazine *Be My Parent* in 1998/9)[33] have a learning difficulty, medical problem and/or physical impairment.

- Older children are more difficult to place, and research shows that they have more difficulty settling within their adoptive families.
- Many children needing families are only placed as part of a sibling group, and this places more complex requirements on the adopters.
- Contact with birth parents is increasingly requested. Not all potential adopters are prepared to face up to the demands of giving love to a child and maintaining some attachment to birth parents.

The brutal truth of the matter is that the children available to adopt are not easy to care for. Contemporary legislation has established that the child's welfare is of paramount importance, and adoptions must respect the influence of religion, ethnicity, culture, language and special needs (physical or learning disabilities). Due to the relatively low numbers of babies in need of adoption, a couple with no children of their own, who wish to start a family through adoption, are much more likely to be able to be able to adopt a child rather than a baby. Sheila Byrne has written about the needs of 'increasing numbers of children who have had very traumatic pasts and who subsequently have major difficulties with attachments, self-esteem, and managing their behaviour.'[34] The children available to adopt in the UK need very special, very committed parents.

In the light of this situation it is not surprising to find that many people look overseas to find a child, frequently a baby, that can become part of their family, without the potential demands of physical, mental or emotional 'baggage.' Some couples seeking a baby from abroad, for example China, may begin with strong emotional motivations to begin a family and to give a needy baby a chance of a more secure future. They may be unaware of the stress placed upon ensuring that the adopted child should grow to have a good understanding of their original cultural heritage. It is a legal requirement that such a couple be assessed by local social services or an adoption agency and they go through the same approval procedure as for a UK adoption.

Children available for adoption from overseas come at a price, with visits to arrange and legal and agency fees to fund. Agencies operating over the Internet advertise the availability of children 'waiting for adoption.' But extreme caution must be exercised in ensuring that all organizations involved are appropriately accredited, and that sufficient information is known about the children so that they are legitimately free for adoption. Inter-country adoptions raise many additional ethical issues, such as the potential for poor parents in poor countries to give up their children, enticed by the comparatively large sums rich potential adoptive parents are prepared to pay. There are also issues of identity faced by children removed from their own countries.

5

Who Wants to Adopt?

A MORI poll (October 2002) has shown that one in four adults 'have either direct experience of adoption or have experienced adoption through a member of their family or a close friend.'[35]

This statistic demonstrates the significance of adoption as a feature of domestic life. A previous survey (October 2001) revealed that 24% of people have considered or would consider adopting. 'The research reveals that amongst those most likely to adopt, single people and co-habiting couples are more likely to consider adopting in the future than married couples, families are twice as likely as childless households, and black people are twice as likely as their white counterparts to consider adoption.'[36] This kind of information formed the backdrop to the Government's position in expanding the range of potential adopters in the Adoption and Children Act (2002).

Setting aside the obvious wisdom of adoption within stepfamilies to safeguard the legal position of children, the people who may want to adopt include those who cannot have children naturally and those who adopt to extend their natural families. Ruth Layzell, a social worker and an adoptive parent, describes adoption as a 'vocation,' a covenantal relationship. 'This is a bond made by choice, in which desire and need weave together to make a relationship. In the covenant, the one with resources dedicates them to the service of the one who needs them and in the process both are enriched.'[37] Layzell thoughtfully uses the word 'painbearer'[38] to describe something of the role of the adoptive parent as they love and provide for a child or children who bear the psychological scars of rejection, scars which may or may not manifest themselves in emotional and behavioural difficulties.

The childless couple may want to adopt. Male infertility accounts for nearly 25% of all failures to conceive. Apart from medical reasons for women being unable to conceive, the average age for first births is now nearly 30, the highest for almost 40 years. A woman's chance of conceiving begins to decline as young as 30 and by 35 it falls away sharply at a rate of 5 to 10 per cent a year, while the risk of miscarriage also increases. It is possible, therefore, that infertility may be discovered when the older couple are in a position to afford fertility treatment to get the longed for baby. The use of reproductive technologies is widespread, and most people will know of someone who has benefited from their use. They are costly, and going through the process, perhaps more than once, can be exceptionally stressful, both physically and emotionally. Some fertility treatments are fraught with ethical dilemmas, for example the legal parenthood of embryos produced with anonymously donated eggs or sperm.

If infertility treatment is unsuccessful, perhaps then adoption will be considered. Maybe, though, adoption would have been a preferable solution from the beginning. Depending on the age and experience of a couple, adopting a young child or children, whilst not offering a genetic match, would offer both the children and the parents a fulfilling way of being a family. It would not be the same as having natural children, but it would be a transforming and creative experience. The sometimes relentless pursuit of trying to have children can be hugely damaging to a couple and is not the Christian ideal, however painful the reality of childlessness. Stephen Post makes this telling comment: 'The successful practice of adoption is proof that parents can transcend the "selfish gene" of the evolutionary psychologists, and that children can prosper without the narrative of a biological lineage (which can easily be idolatrous).'[39] Layzell encapsulates the tension between pain and gain for the childless couple adopting when she says: 'In adoption, it is the adopters who make the promise to be parents to children who have already suffered and the adopters who bear the burden of responsibility in the relationship. It is their desire to become parents which initiates the family, their love which must bear the burden of the losses which both they and their children bring, and their strength which must sustain the relationship.'[40]

Maybe, though, adoption would have been a preferable solution from the beginning

The childless couple may not be married, and issues of permanence and stability of relationship need to be addressed. In the debate preceding the passing of the legislation, the Christian Institute was one group that spoke out against any non-married couple adopting children. They cited the inherent instability of cohabiting couples (83% break up within 10 years[41]) as their primary motivation, predicting further emotional upset for the child adopted into this uncommitted partnership. Their poster campaign showed a photograph of a gay couple from Essex, who adopted two babies from America, and asked the reader: 'If you died who would they give your children to?' The Institute regards it as 'social engineering'[42] to place children for adoption with un-married people.

A similar position, though less inflammatory, was taken by the CARE organization and Roman Catholic adoption agencies. In a letter to *The Guardian* newspaper the director of the Catholic Children's Society (Westminster) said: 'The key thing about adoption is the total commitment required of the couple to the child. One of the best ways of judging whether a couple can do this is if they have made such a commitment to each other.'[43]

Whilst a stable, married couple can, and usually does, provide an excellent environment for adopted children, one must not forget that children available for adoption are often born to married couples and that marriage in itself is no guarantee of good parenting. The fact remains that there are embedded requirements upon social workers in the Adoption and Children Act to assess both 'suitability' and 'permanence of relationship.' It is social workers and adoption agencies that have the final say over who may adopt.

Single people have been able to adopt children for some time. Agencies are often on the lookout for single carers, with professional childcare experience, or older people as adopters for children with particular emotional, mental or physical difficulties. Before the new 2002 Act, one person within an unmarried couple could adopt, leaving the partner with no legal rights if the relationship broke down. The Act permits joint adoption of a child, or children, despite a couple being unmarried, and therefore permits custody and access agreements to be made appropriately, should the relationship break down.

Previously unmentioned in this discussion about who may want to adopt, are married couples with children. In no way does the legislation make it any easier for this group. In *all* cases the work of social workers is to ensure that the child's welfare is paramount and that they will be placed into an environment best suited to their needs. It is, however, this group of couples who need to hear about the plight of children in care most of all. The experience of having 'been there and done that' is something that can be offered to other children.

There is a myth about the type of 'ideal adopter.' 'The traditional image, still held by many, of *ideal* adopters as young, married, infertile couples, wishing to replace by adoption the child they have not been able to conceive "naturally" is no longer accurate or helpful.'[44] 'There is a common conception that the ideal adoptive unit would consist of a married couple with no dependent children (but preferably with some child care experience), where one partner is able to be at home to offer full-time care to the adopted child. Such units do, however, form an increasingly small proportion of the population.'[45]

These statements come from BAAF and would encourage some working couples with existing families to come forward, whilst not restricting the important work that agencies do with childless couples or single people. The process is not, however, infallible and the press has taken offence at some of the judgments made. One journalist wrote: 'Parents have been turned down for being too fat, too middle class, having too many books or not enough sex, being too old, the wrong colour, or for showing insufficient grief about their infertility.'[46] Such stories are at odds with some of the official words used: 'The most important factor in determining whether potential adopters will be able to be effective adoptive parents appears to be the extent to which their previous life experience has equipped them for this task.'[47]

Who Takes the Decision?

6

Christian organizations have always been at the forefront of caring for under-privileged children, and the earliest adoption agencies were Christian in their foundation.

Barnardo's opened its first home in London in 1870; NCH began as 'The Children's Home' founded by three Methodist men in 1869; and The Children's Society was founded as 'The Church of England Central Society for Providing Homes for Waifs and Strays' in 1881. One of the many Roman Catholic agencies, The Catholic Children's Society (Westminster), traces its origins to 1859 as the Crusade of Rescue, running homes for destitute children in London. Local authorities have regulated independent or voluntary adoption agencies such as these since 1939, with local authorities becoming agencies themselves in 1988.

For those who want to adopt, the assessment process begins with an initial interview between the adoption agency and the prospective adopter(s). A series of interviews with the allocated social worker will follow where couples are seen together and individually. There may also be small group work, where prospective adopters have a chance to meet adoptive parents or explore case studies about different children available for adoption and the issues involved. Discussions will range from the stability of the adopter(s) within their own family or network of relationships, to finances, age, educational background, religion, health and expectations, through to the type of child preferred: gender, age, health, emotional and mental stability, contact with birth parents and so on. The Department of Health adds to this discussion: 'The parenting capacity of the prospective adopter/s to meet the developmental needs of the child' and 'the developmental capacity of the adoptive parent/s to meet the child's needs over time.'[48] On completion of the process, the prospective adopter(s) names are submitted to the agency's adoption panel for approval, or otherwise.

Two quotations from sources written 24 years apart reflect the transition in the thinking of social workers. In 1977, Barbara Tizard wrote: 'In some circles the motivation of adopters is often considered suspect. If infertile, they are suspected of having unresolved psychological problems about inability to bear a child, if they have children already they are suspected of acting from charitable or political motives.'[49] In 2001, the Department of Health phrased it like this: 'The first principle in matching children with adoptive parents is to secure the best possible developmental outcomes for children over the course of their childhood and into adulthood. A pro-active and positive recruitment strategy is essential to provide for sufficient numbers and range of adopters to be recruited to allow choice in the placement of children.'[50]

Adoption agencies are no longer characterized as charitable organizations but rather as providers of an approval service to prospective parents and seekers of temporary (foster) or permanent (adoptive) parents for children. Matching the needs of a child to the capability of the parent(s) is the demanding work of social workers and especially so at a time when the numbers of children in care are so high and Government officials are measuring success rates critically. It is also the area open to most public debate and to criticism from some Christian organizations.

Matching the needs of a child to the capability of the parent(s) is the demanding work of social workers

Previously, linking parent with child was a physical and intellectual matching process. Now parents are selected because of evidence for parenting potential established during a psychosocial investigation. An interesting point has been raised about power, and the specific power of the adoption panel to decide on the ultimate suitability of a person(s) to be an adoptive parent. Within most agencies a mix of professional (medical, legal, social workers, agency managers) and experienced 'lay' people (adoptive parent, adopted person, and clergy, especially for Christian agencies) will work together on the adoption panel. 'The assessment process has been compared to an obstacle course when applicants can feel as if they jump through hoops, giving the "right" answers that will validate them as people and potential parents and ultimately convince those involved to allow them the possibility of their longed for child.'[51] One prospective adopter phrased it like this: 'If you get pregnant, even if it has taken time to come to that decision and for it to happen, once it's done there's not much you can do apart from wait for it to be born. But when going through a lengthy process of other people questioning your lifestyle, relationship and personality it can really make you begin to doubt that you have anything to offer.'[52] This contemporary view suggests that the potential adoptive parent can still be as misunderstood by social workers, as they were in 1977, when Tizard was writing.

Approval Criteria

Each agency has the right to operate within its own guidelines, which may exclude a subset of the spectrum of adults that could generally be approved for adoption, that is, agencies can have their own approval criteria. The Department of Health has written that potential 'applicants will be considered in terms of their capacity to look after children in a safe and responsible way that meets their developmental needs. Where agencies have specific eligibility criteria *eg* because the agency had particular religious beliefs, applicants will be told what these are and, if necessary, be referred to another agency. People will not be *automatically* excluded on the grounds of age, health or other factors, except in the case of certain criminal convictions.'[53]

Approval criteria vary considerably between the Christian agencies. In a recent seminar a game of 'match the approval criteria with the agency' was played, using actual criteria from Anglican, Methodist, Non-Conformist, Roman Catholic and a County Council's adoption policies. No team of participants was able to combine criteria with agency successfully, proving how general and indistinct agencies are from one another, despite having a Christian foundation. The approval criteria available introduced the main strengths, weaknesses, opportunities and threats to the whole notion of family and adoption from a Christian viewpoint. It was interesting to notice which agencies mentioned marital status or sexual orientation and which mentioned any specific Christian motivation as a basis for their criteria. Apart from meeting the essential requirements of legislation, each agency placed stress on different criteria. Not having fertility treatment was relevant to all; health issues were critical for some; not smacking was important in one instance and for others, their inclusion of applications from single or gay people was made explicit within their opening statements. Some Roman Catholic agencies, even with their strong doctrine of family and marriage, have taken the word 'Catholic' out of their name to de-focus from what may be perceived as an excluding stance. Adoptive parents are so urgently needed that Christian agencies are struggling to attract the number of applications they desire. Their motivation is purely honourable, but there is room to question their presentation when it seems that, in most instances, mention of Christian values is left in the small print.

In the light of the latest legislation, the workload of adoption agencies is destined to increase. Christian agencies and local authority agencies (whose approval criteria are decided by legislation alone) do not necessarily work with different groups of people. The approval criteria for many Christian agencies are indistinguishable from secular agencies. The question needs to be asked 'Is this right?' Should Christian tradition and biblical insights better inform the practise of who should or should not be approved? The drive to increase the 'numbers and range of adopters'[54] makes the approval of more people an imperative, and every effort needs to be made to broaden the range and numbers of people coming through the approval process. Approval is the area most hotly debated in contemporary discussions on adoption.

The debate about who should be able to be an adopter reached fever pitch in the run up to the passing of the Adoption and Children Act (2002). This Act brought in vital new aspects of policy and practice, but the issue that excited the press and some Christian organizations was the matter of adoption by unmarried couples or single people. The view of BAAF, and presumably that of many silent Christian adoption agencies, was that: 'If we restrict joint adoption to married couples we can only reduce the opportunity for children to find adoptive parents—there is already a shortage of adopters for many groups of children.'[55]

Do Christian values and motives make a real difference to the way Christian adoption agencies work?

To summarize: the adoption panel of each adoption agency has the responsibility for deciding who can adopt. Whereas at one time adoptive parents could say to their child that he or she had been chosen by them, now all the selection is done by the agency. The role of the social worker for the child and the social worker for the approved adoptive parent(s) is key. In many ways, Christian adoption agencies feel that it is inappropriate to be explicit about their religious conviction, and any underlying theology motivating their work is hidden from the public eye. I want to ask questions about this position: Do Christian values and motives make a real difference to the way Christian adoption agencies work and the judgments they make? If it does make a difference to be Christian, then why are the agencies afraid to be specific about what they do and why?

Creating the Right Family: An Eschatological Model of Family 7

Research has shown that the future of children who remain in care is likely to be socially and emotionally chaotic.

Children who are adopted, especially if this is done in the early years, can often achieve their full potential and make a positive contribution to society. Rarely can individual acts make a significant difference in issues of social or environmental justice, but through adoption individual actions make a huge difference to the life of a child.

Specific individual actions and choices affecting adoption inevitably include those related to abortion. The CARE organization has 150 independent centres throughout the UK offering non-directional counselling to pregnant women to help them plan their future, informing women as to the realities of contemporary adoption and abortion. This is one effective way in which Christian values can make a demonstrable difference to the future life of a child.

Through adoption individual actions make a huge difference to the life of a child

Christ was not ambivalent about children or families. Both Old and New Testaments depict families as entities with huge potential to love and nurture. This was Jesus' personal experience. In the early church, Christian families had a particularly demanding task to model what God wanted within families, with their radical openness to all regardless of gender, age or social class. Christian households existed within society to transform the conventional model and offer a paradigm for family at odds with what society expected.

The Bible teaches Christians to uphold the permanence of marriage and to bring up children within this stable unit. It also promotes models of being family that go beyond blood ties, and extends the reaches of the family to include the stranger and the outcast. Once the stranger is drawn into the family, then the individual is no longer 'strange' and the outsider is now in. The Bible also teaches us about God's adoption of us as his children. The principles of adoption and inclusivity should be embedded within an understanding of Christian family. Living with these kingdom values within the family is not easy, but it is a step closer towards the experience of the family of the age to come where the only bonds are those of love.[56]

Offering a New Paradigm

Adoption is a way of introducing a new member into an existing household. It is a way of offering all that is good about Christian family life to someone who may otherwise know nothing about unconditional love, security and stability. It involves selfless sacrifice, time and money. This is familiar territory to Christ but not necessarily to those who follow him. Christians who do this will become a family that is shaped by the adopted individual. Behaviour may or may not be acceptable within home or church contexts. Achievement may or may not be demonstrated in those terms classically valued by non-Christian and Christian alike. The ability to conform to the 'rosy image' of family may be difficult but not impossible. This new family offers a paradigm of Christian values to society.

This is familiar territory to Christ but not necessarily to those who follow him

What then of those whose remit it is to find adopters? Adoption agencies should be encouraged to be more explicit about the Christian basis for their important work. This does not imply that those who are approved will be exclusively Christian or married or heterosexual. Placing the needs of the children uppermost does not prevent an agency from defining its position as Christian and need not be regarded as off-putting to potential adopters. Churches are the obvious places for adoption agencies to find Christian couples and families who may be prepared to offer themselves as adopters. This would raise the profile of the need of the children, reinforce the role of the Christian family in caring for children and promote an agency's work. The minister whose church included regular contact with an adoption agency would be able to preach and teach Christian understanding of what it is to be a family and encourage members to offer a new paradigm of family to society, with or without additional adopted members. For the Christian family itself, the needs of children in care and the ability to offer transforming love, make their own appeals.

Conclusions

8

Some families are natural and some are created.

Adoption legislation exists so that those families that are created, either from scratch or by extension, are stable, secure and permanent environments within which to bring up children.

It is my opinion that a biblical view of adoption should make children the priority, rather than the issue of who should be able to adopt them. The biblical model of what it is to be family is far broader than the nuclear family image we uphold as being the Christian family. The regard of society for what can be inherited, and for blood ties, has taken precedence over ties of love. From a biblical viewpoint, the institution of marriage represents God's ideal for those who would be adoptive parents. Yet as Christians we need to accept that not enough married couples are willing to consider adoption, that not all married couples who are willing are suitable parents for adopted children, and the need of children is so urgent that marriage should not be a barrier to those considered suitable on every other ground. Some children simply need someone to love them. The least desirable situation is for the numbers of children without permanent families to continue to be so high.

I have argued in this booklet that the plight of children waiting for adoption is a challenge to the church. The challenge is to Christian individuals and families, Christian ministers, Christian adoption agencies and those Christian organizations who speak out in the public arena.

- The challenge to Christian individuals and families is to question how they best serve children. What expectations do we have of our children? What constitutes being a 'good' Christian family? How can our parenting skills be offered to children who are not our own?

- The challenge to Christian ministers is to grow in a biblical understanding of what the family is and what it could be. In preaching about outreach and care for those in our community, let us preach about the vocation of adoption and celebrate our own adoption as children of God. Let us build links with local adoption agencies and actively pray for social workers working in this demanding field. Let us work to support and embrace the parents of children whose needs and behaviours are difficult to cope with.

- The challenge to Christian adoption agencies is to reflect theologically upon their work and to understand their mission and responsibility in this area. Agencies need to have a clear presentation of who they can approve and why, and to understand the Christian basis for the decisions they are making.

- And finally, the challenge to Christian organizations who have a political voice is to strike a positive note: 'Let us find people to be adopters! Let us find homes for children in care!' Let us set aside the negativity of speaking against those who do not model God's ideal for family life and offer Christian solutions to the new legislation.

I have proposed a new model for being family, an eschatological model where the ties and bonds of love are more valued than the ties and bonds of blood. The model is a response to Old and New Testament examples of kinship, household and family of faith, drawing in and offering hospitality to the stranger. Christians are therefore called to offer physical, emotional and spiritual security to both natural and adopted children. It is a high calling indeed.

Bibliography

British Agencies for Adoption and Fostering, *Linking Children with Adoptive Parents* (London: BAAF, 2000)

BAAF, *Adoption and Fostering Briefing on the Adoption and Children Bill for the House of Commons*, 2nd Reading—29 October 2001

Barker, Sylvia *et al*, *Preparing for Permanence: Assessment—Points to consider for those assessing potential adopters and foster carers*, (London: BAAF, 1998)

Barton, Stephen C (ed), *The Family in Theological Perspective*, (Edinburgh: T & T Clark, 1996)

Barton, Stephen C, *Life Together: Family, Sexuality and Community in the New Testament and Today* (Edinburgh; New York: T & T Clark, 2001)

Bridger, Francis, *Celebrating the Family: A Critique of the BSR Report 'Something to Celebrate'* (Grove Ethics booklet E 99a)

Byrne, Sheila, *Linking and Introductions: Helping children join adoptive families* (London: BAAF, 2000)

Church of England Board of Social Responsibility, *Something to Celebrate: Valuing Families in Church and Society* (London: Church House Publishing, 1995)

Department of Health, Local Authority Circular (LAC(98)20)

Department of Health, *Draft Practice Guidance to Support the National Adoption Standards for England—Issued for Consultation*

Department of Health, *National Adoption Standards for England*, August 2001

Methodist Statement on 'A Christian Understanding of Family Life, The Single Person and Marriage'—Adopted by the Methodist Conference of 1992

Hays, Richard B, *The Moral Vision of the New Testament—A Contemporary Introduction to New Testament Ethics* (Edinburgh: T & T Clark, 1996)

Hicks, Stephen and McDermott, Janet (eds), *Lesbian and Gay Fostering and Adoption—Extraordinary Yet Ordinary* (London: Jessica Kingsley Publishers, 1999)

Hill, Malcolm and Shaw, Martin (eds), *Signposts in Adoption: Policy, practice and research issues* (London: British Agency for Adoption and Fostering, 1998)

Layzell, Ruth, *Adoption is for Life, Not Just for a Crisis* (Cambridge: Grove Pastoral booklet P 77)

Post, Stephen G, *More Lasting Unions—Christianity, the Family and Society* (Grand Rapids, Michigan: Eerdmans, 2000)

Scott, James M, *Adoption as Sons of God* (Tubingen: J C Mohr (Paul Siebeck), 1992)

Tizard, Barbara, *Adoption—A Second Chance* (London: Open Books, 1977)

Notes

1   Department of Health, 'Children Looked After by Local Authorities—Year Ending 31 March 2001, England,' http://www.doh.gov.uk/public/cla2001.htm (28 April 2003). An additional 12% of children were 'placed with parents,' 6% had been adopted and the remainder were in a mixture of residential settings including Children's Homes and secure units.

2   BAAF, 'MORI Survey Shatters Stereotypes of Potential Adopters,' 8 October 2001, http://www.morimrc.ie/polls/2001/baaf.shtml (5 November 2002).

3   *Adoption and Children Act 2002*—Chapter 38, paragraph 45, http://www.hmso.gov.uk/acts/acts2002/20020038.htm (10 December 2002).

4   Stephen C Barton, 'Biblical Hermeneutics and the Family, Barton (ed), *The Family in Theological Perspective*, p 20.

5   Ibid.

6   James Francis, 'Children and Childhood in the New Testament' in Barton (ed), *The Family in Theological Perspective*, pp 65–85.

7   James D G Dunn, 'The Household Rules in the New Testament' in Barton (ed), *The Family in Theological Perspective*, pp 43–63.

8   James M Scott, *Adoption as Sons of God*, p 55.

9   Ibid, p 121.

10 Ibid, p 149.

11 Ibid, p 174.

12 Anthony Fletcher, 'The Family, Marriage and the Upbringing of Children in Protestant England' in Barton (ed), *The Family in Theological Perspective*, pp 107–128.

13 Ibid, p 116.

14 Ibid, p 119.

15 Ibid, p 127.

16 Francis Bridger, *Celebrating the Family*, p 10.

17 Church of England Board of Social Responsibility, *Something to Celebrate*, p 62.

18 Methodist Statement on *'A Christian Understanding of Family Life.'*

19 *Something to Celebrate*, p 82. Francis Bridger correctly drew attention to the theological and historical weaknesses of this report in his Grove booklet *Celebrating the Family*. Whilst the debate continues, however, it is imperative that children are not excluded from church or family life.

20 Jon Davies, *A Preferential Option for the Family*, pp 219–236.

21 Ibid.

22 Gerard Loughlin, 'The Want of Family in Post-Modernity' in Barton (ed), *The Family in Theological Perspective*, p 320.

23 Stephen G Post, *More Lasting Unions*, p 124.

24 Kate Kellaway, 'And baby makes three?' *The Observer*, Sunday 7 January 2001 http://www.observer.co.uk/review/story/0,6903,418747,00.html (8 October 2002).

25 John Triseliotis, 'Adoption—evolution or revolution?' in Hill and Shaw (eds), *Signposts in Adoption*, pp 56–70.

26 BAAF, *Adoption and Fostering Briefing*.

27 Barbara Tizard, *Adoption—A Second Chance*, p 6.

28 Table H, Looked after children adopted during the years ending 31 March 1997 to 2001, www.doh.gov.uk/public/cla2001/cla2001tableh.xls (28 April 2003).

29 Cited in BAAF, 'MORI Survey Shatters Stereotypes of Potential Adopters,' 8 October 2001, http://www.morimrc.ie/polls/2001/baaf.shtml (5 November 2002).

30 MORI—UK Attitudes to Adoption, 15 October 2002, http://www.morimrc.ie/polls/2002/baaf.shtml (5 November 2002).

31 Alice Thomson, 'Adoption Bill has become gays' battlefield,' *Daily Telegraph*, 5 November 2002.

32 Department of Health, Local Authority Circular (LAC(98)20), paragraph 5.

33 BAAF, *Linking Children with Adoptive Parents* (London: BAAF, 2000) p 12.

34 Sheila Byrne, *Linking and Introductions,* pp 5–6.

35 MORI—UK Attitudes to Adoption, 15 October 2002, http://www.morimrc.ie/polls/2002/baaf.shtml (5 November 2002).

36 BAAF, 'MORI Survey Shatters Stereotypes.'

37 Ruth Layzell, *Adoption is for Life,* p 19.

38 Originally used by J Cotter, *Healing—More or Less* (Sheffield: Cairns Publications, 1990) p 17.

39 Stephen G Post, *More Lasting Unions,* p 121.

40 Ruth Layzell, *Adoption is for Life,* p 19.

41 Work of Berthoud and Gershuny (2000) quoted by The Christian Institute—'Adoption Law: If you died, who would they give your children to?' http://www.christian.org.uk/html-publications/adoption_poster.htm (5 November 2002).

42 The Christian Institute *ibid.*

43 Letter to *The Guardian,* J M Richards, Director, The Catholic Children's Society (Westminster) 29 October 2001 http://www.cathchild.org.uk/gu291001.html (20 December 2002).

44 BAAF, *Linking Children with Adoptive Parents,* p 2.

45 Ibid, p 17.

46 Kate Kellaway, 'And baby makes three?'

47 BAAF, *Linking Children with Adoptive Parents,* p 17.

48 Department of Health, *Draft Practice Guidance.*

49 Barbara Tizard, *Adoption,* p 240.

50 Department of Health, *Draft Practice Guidance,* paragraph 26.

51 Sylvia Barker *et al, Preparing for Permanence,* p 2.

52 Expressed by one lesbian partner in Hicks, and McDermott (eds), *Lesbian and Gay Fostering and Adoption,* p 177.

53 Department of Health, *National Adoption Standards for England,* August 2001.

54 Department of Health, *Draft Practice Guidance,* para 26.

55 BAAF, *Adoption and Fostering Briefing.*

56 This view is expanded by Gerard Loughlin in 'The Want of Family in Post-Modernity' in Barton (ed), *The Family in Theological Perspective,* pp 307–327.